Teaching Stems-Another Branch of Reading Comprehension

5th Grade and Up

by

Sheila Statham Thompson

Cover illustrated by Pamela Statham Lawless

Bloomington, IN  Milton Keynes, UK

authorHOUSE®

AuthorHouse™
1663 Liberty Drive, Suite 200
Bloomington, IN 47403
www.authorhouse.com
Phone: 1-800-839-8640

AuthorHouse™ UK Ltd.
500 Avebury Boulevard
Central Milton Keynes, MK9 2BE
www.authorhouse.co.uk
Phone: 08001974150

First published by AuthorHouse 10/2/2006

ISBN: 1-4259-6429-X (sc)

Printed in the United States of America
Bloomington, Indiana

This book is printed on acid-free paper.

Table of Contents

Contents and How to Use This Book
Sample Lesson Plan
Stems' Practice Lesson
Stems' Practice Test
Stems' Practice Test with Answers
Stems #1
Stems' #1 Test
Stems #2
Stems' #2 Test
Stems #3
Stems' #3 Test
Stem Bingo (Lessons 1-3)
Bingo Calling Cards with Definitions
    (Lessons 1-3)
Stems #4
Stems' #4 Test
Stems #5
Stems' #5 Test
Stems #6
Stems' #6 Test
Stem Bingo (Lessons 4-6)
Bingo Calling Cards with Definitions
    (Lessons 4-6)
Stems #7
Stems' #7 Test
Stems #8
Stems' #8 Test
Stems #9
Stems' #9 Test
Stem Bingo (Lessons 7-9)
Bingo Calling Cards with Definitions
    (Lessons 7-9)
Stems #10
Stems' #10 Test
Stems #11
Stems' #11 Test
Stems #12
Stems' #12 Test
Stem Bingo (Lessons 10-12)
Bingo Calling Cards with Definitions
    (Lessons 10-12)
Stems #13
Stems' #13 Test
Stems #14
Stems' #14 Test
Stems #15

Stems' #15 Test
Stem Bingo (Lessons 13-15)
Bingo Calling Cards with Definitions
    (Lessons 13-15)
Stems #16
Stems' #16 Test
Stems #17
Stems' #17 Test
Stems #18
Stems' #18 Test
Stem Bingo (Lessons 16-18)
Bingo Calling Cards with Definitions
    (Lessons 16-18)
Stems #19
Stems' #19 Test
Stems #20
Stems' #20 Test
Stems # 21
Stems' #21 Test
Stem Bingo (Lessons 19-21)
Bingo Calling Cards with Definitions
    (Lessons 19-21)
Stems #22
Stems' #22 Test
Stems #23
Stems' #23 Test
Stems #24
Stems' #24 Test
Stem Bingo (Lessons 22-24)
Bingo Calling Cards with Definitions
    (Lessons 22-24)
Stems #25
Stems' #25 Test
Stems #26
Stems' #26 Test
Stems #27
Stems' #27 Test
Stem Bingo (Lessons 25-27)
Bingo Calling Cards with Definitions
    (Lessons 25-27)
Stems #28
Stems' #28 Test
Stems #29
Stems' #29 Test
Stems #30
Stems' #30 Test

Stem Bingo (Lessons 28-30)
Bingo Calling Cards with Definitions
    (Lessons 28-30)
Stems #31
Stems' #31 Test
Stems #32
Stems' #32 Test
Stems #33
Stems' #33 Test
Stem Bingo (Lessons 31-33)
Bingo Calling Cards with Definitions
    (Lessons 31-33)
Stems #34
Stems' #34 Test

Stems #35
Stems' #35 Test
Stems #36
Stems' #36 Test
Stem Bingo (Lessons 34-36)
Bingo Calling Cards with Definitions
    (Lessons 34-36)
Appendix
Stem Form
Stem Bingo
Stem Tests' Answers
Bibliography

Contents

1 Stem Practice Lesson
36 Stem Lessons with Tests
12 Stem Bingo Games
1 Stem Form
1 Stem Bingo Form
1 Answer Key

How to Use This Book

There are three basic parts to this book:
                Stem Lessons,
                Stem Tests, and
                Stem Bingo games.
This book is designed to give one stem lesson per week.

1. Stems = Each stem lesson introduces 10 new stems, their meaning, and a word example for each stem. Make a transparency of this stem page. Also, make a copy for each student of the *Stem Form*, front and back, which is found in the Appendix. This form is used for the students to copy their stem lessons. (Make a transparency of the *Stems' Practice Lesson* to use to explain how each lesson works.)

2. Stem Test = Make a copy of the stem test for each student. They will define the 10 stems and then find the meaning of the unusual words by using the meaning of the stems. Most of the word's definitions contain the exact stem definition while some contain a synonym. (Make a transparency of the *Stems' Practice Lesson* to use to explain how each lesson works.)

3. Stem Bingo = There is a bingo game designed for every third lesson. The bingo games can be used as a lesson by themself or they can be used in addition to the weekly lesson. Make a transparency of the *Stem Bingo* lesson. Make copies of the Stem Bingo card, front and back, which can be found in the Appendix. Have the students copy the stems onto their bingo card. Six of the stems will not be used. Make a card stock copy of the *Bingo Calling Cards with Definitions* and cut them apart. Provide cubes to cover the stems when called out.

Sample Lesson Plan

Before the first lesson is given, be sure to use the practice lesson to explain how the lessons work.

Monday:
- ✓ Introduce stems, meaning, and the word examples.

Tuesday, Wednesday, and Thursday:
- ✓ Review the stems.
    - o Revisit the transparency.
    - o Use flash cards with the whole class.
    - o Allow students to make their own set of flash cards.
    - o Give students five minutes to study on their own.
    - o Allow students to make a set of cards for the stems and a set of cards for the meanings and then play match.
    - o Give practice test.
    - o List other words with the stems. (The stems can be at the beginning, in the middle, or at the end of the word.)

Friday:
- ✓ Give test.

After the third lesson:
- ✓ Play bingo.
    - o Use it as another lesson.
    - o Use it along with the fourth lesson.

Stems' Practice Lesson

Stem	Meaning	Word Example
digit	finger	digital
atom	vapor	atomic
hemi	half	hemisphere
orb	circle	orbit
lin	line	linear
grade	step	gradual
multi	many	multicultural
ob	against	object
ign	fire	ignition
foli	leaf	folium

Stems' Practice Test

A. Write the meaning of each stem in the box.

Stem	Meaning
1. foli	
2. atom	
3. orb	
4. multi	
5. ign	
6. lin	
7. hemi	
8. ob	
9. grade	
10. digit	

B. Write the alphabet of the definition beside the correct word.

Word	Definition
____ 1. orbicular	a. indirect, evasive, or opposite
____ 2. ignite	b. division into fingerlike parts.
____ 3. retrograde	c. circular or spherical
____ 4. diatomic	d. direct descent or direct line from a particular ancestor
____ 5. oblique	e. a cluster of leaves.
____ 6. lineage	f. moving or stepping backward
____ 7. foliage	g. pain affecting one half of the body
____ 8. multilateral	h. to set fire to
____ 9. digitations	i. having many sides
____ 10. hemialgia	j. made up of two atoms

4

Stems' Practice Test with Answers

A. Write the meaning of each stem in the box.

Stem	Meaning
1. foli	leaf
2. atom	vapor
3. orb	circle
4. multi	many
5. ign	fire
6. lin	line
7. hemi	half
8. ob	against
9. grade	step
10. digit	finger

B. Write the alphabet of the definition beside the correct word.

Word	Definition
_c_ 1. orbicular	a. indirect, evasive, or opposite
_h_ 2. ignite	b. division into fingerlike parts.
_f_ 3. retrograde	c. circular or spherical
_j_ 4. diatomic	d. direct descent or direct line from a particular ancestor
_a_ 5. oblique	e. a cluster of leaves.
_d_ 6. lineage	f. moving or stepping backward
_e_ 7. foliage	g. pain affecting one half of the body
_i_ 8. multilateral	h. to set fire to
_b_ 9. digitations	i. having many sides
_g_ 10. hemialgia	j. made up of two atoms

Stems #1

STEM	MEANING	WORD EXAMPLE
sol	sun	solar
dis	away	dismiss
biblio	book	bibliography
ish	like	greenish
less	without	bootless
grav	heavy	aggravate
rub	red	ruby
xylo	wood	xylophone
atmo	vapor	atmosphere
monger	seller	fishmonger

Stems' #1 Test

Name _____ Period ____ Date _____

A. Write the meaning of the following stems.

Stem	Meaning
1. less	
2. monger	
3. grav	
4. dis	
5. biblio	
6. sol	
7. xylo	
8. atmo	
9. rub	
10. ish	

B. Write the alphabet of the definition beside the correct word.

Words	Definitions
____ 1. motherless	a. the part of a charge or an accusation that weighs heavily against the accuses
____ 2. atmometer	b. An engraving on wood
____ 3. rubescent	c. an instrument that measures the rate of water evaporation
____ 4. warmonger	d. a dread of books
____ 5. bibliophobia	e. either of two times of the year when the sun is at its greatest distance from the celestial equator
____ 6. gravamen	f. easily or likely to be nauseated or sickened
____ 7. solstice	g. one who tries to sell the idea or attempts to stir up a war
____ 8. squeamish	h. one without a mother
____ 9. disperse	i. to drive away or scatter in different directions
____ 10. xylem	j. turning red

Stems #2

Stem	Meaning	Word Example
sym	together	symmetry
mis	bad	miser
syn	together	synthetic
pre	before	predict
tri	three	tripod
sub	under	submarine
post	after	postscript
un	not	unearned
semi	half	semicircle
super	over	supernatural

Stems' #2 Test

A. Write the meaning of the following stems.

Stem	Meaning
1. post	
2. mis	
3. pre	
4. un	
5. semi	
6. tri	
7. sub	
8. sym	
9. super	
10. syn	

B. Write the alphabet of the definition beside the correct word.

Words

_____ 1. symposium

_____ 2. subordinate

_____ 3. premonition

_____ 4. unequal

_____ 5. postlude

_____ 6. supervise

_____ 7. misfortune

_____ 8. semitone

_____ 9. triceratops

_____ 10. synchronize

Definitions

a. a warning in advance or before an event or happening

b. to occur together, in unison

c. bad or ill luck

d. a concluding or ending piece, after the final chapter or phase

e. coming together for a meeting or conference for discussion of a topic or the posing of a question

f. an interval equal to a half tone in the standard diatonic scale

g. a herbivorous dinosaur having three horns

h. under the authority or control of another

i. to have charge of or direction over

j. not the same in any measurable aspect

Stems #3

Stem	Meaning	Word Example
inter	between	interject
ante	before	antepenult
bi	two	bimonthly
com	together	combo
anti	against	antibody
mal	bad	malady
de	down	deduct
equi	equal	equilateral
circum	around	circus
extra	beyond	extrovert

Stems' #3 Test

Name _____ Period _____ Date _____

A. Write the meaning of the following stems.

Stem	Meaning
1. ante	
2. anti	
3. bi	
4. circum	
5. com	
6. de	
7. equi	
8. extra	
9. inter	
10. mal	

B. Write the alphabet of the definition beside the correct word.

Words

_____ 1. bicuspid

_____ 2. denounce

_____ 3. interlude

_____ 4. equiponderant

_____ 5. antebellum

_____ 6. circumspect

_____ 7. extravagant

_____ 8. malign

_____ 9. comity

_____ 10. antithesis

Definitions

a. to announce formerly the termination of someone or the ending of their employment

b. careful to consider all circumstances and possible consequences

c. bad in nature, influence or effort

d. having or ending in two points

e. equally balanced

f. a friendly social atmosphere with everyone together

g. going beyond the limits of reasons or necessity

h. a musical composition inserted between the parts of a longer composition

i. existing before a war such as the Civil War

j. the exact opposite, going against the other

Stem Bingo (Lessons 1–3)

sol	sym	inter
dis	mis	ante
biblio	syn	bi
ish	pre	com
less	tri	anti
grav	sub	mal
rub	post	de
xylo	un	equi
atmo	semi	circum
monger	super	extra

Randomly copy one of these stems in each box on your bingo card. Six will not be used.

Copy the Stems Bingo form on the front and back of a piece of paper so the students will have two forms.

Bingo Calling Cards with Definitions
(Lessons 1-3)

sun = sol	together = sym	between = inter
away = dis	bad = mis	before = ante
book = biblio	together = syn	two = bi
like = ish	before = pre	together = com
without = less	three = tri	against = anti
heavy = grav	under = sub	bad = mal
red = rub	after = post	down = de
wood = xylo	not = un	equal = equi
vapor = atmo	half = semi	around = circum
seller = monger	over = super	beyond = extra

Make a copy of this card and cut out the boxes. Shuffle the cards and call out the definitions.

Stems #4

STEM	MEANING	WORD EXAMPLE
con	together	confederate
intra	within	intravenous
intro	into	introvert
non	not	nonprofit
aqua	water	aquatic
logy	science	mythology
neo	new	neon
miss	send	dismiss
cent	one hundred	centipede
cise	cut	incisive

Stems' #4 Test

Name _____ Period _____ Date _____

A. Write the meaning of the following stems.

Stem	Meaning
1. neo	
2. intra	
3. cent	
4. con	
5. cise	
6. aqua	
7. miss	
8. logy	
9. intro	
10. non	

B. Write the alphabet of the definition beside the correct word.

Words	Definitions
_____ 1. incisors	a. an officer commanding a Roman century
_____ 2. semiaquatic	b. a substance discharged or sent into the air
_____ 3. introject	c. the part of speech that puts together words, phrases, clauses, or sentences.
_____ 4. centurion	d. existing or occurring within a state
_____ 5. emission	e. a front tooth adapted for cutting
_____ 6. nonchalant	f. belonging to an earlier age, not new
_____ 7. conjunction	g. the scientific study of human beings in relations to their culture
_____ 8. neolithic	h. growing equally well in or adjacent to water
_____ 9. intrastate	i. seeming to be coolly not concerned
_____ 10. anthropology	j. to incorporate into one's own self unconsciously

Stems #5

Stem	Meaning	Word Example
auto	self	autograph
archy	government	monarchy
ician	specialist	beautician
cap	take	captive
dict	say	predict
anthropo	man	anthropoid
bio	life	biography
mono	one	monotone
port	carry	transport
bell	war	antebellum

Stems' #5 Test

A. Write the meaning of the following stems.

Stem	Meaning
1. mono	
2. archy	
3. cap	
4. ician	
5. auto	
6. anthropo	
7. bell	
8. dict	
9. port	
10. bio	

B. Write the alphabet of the definition beside the correct word.

Words	Definitions
_____ 1. contradict	a. a mathematic specialist
_____ 2. biogenesis	b. involving or affecting one eye
_____ 3. statistician	c. warlike in manner or temperament
_____ 4. monocular	d. to send out or to carry away
_____ 5. captivate	e. a delusion where a man believes he has become a wolf
_____ 6. automation	f. to assert or say the opposite of an action or another statement
_____ 7. deport	g. social organization marked by the supremacy of the father in the clan or family, a government run by a male person
_____ 8. bellicose	h. the development of life from preexisting life
_____ 9. lycanthropy	i. to seize or take by special charm
_____ 10. patriarchy	j. the technique of making an apparatus that operates by its self

17

Stems #6

Stem	Meaning	Word Example
ard	always	coward
scribe	write	describe
cede	go	precede
penta	five	pentagon
itis	infection	tonsillitis
ad	to	adhesive
cide	kill	herbicide
cred	believe	credit
viv	life	viva
audi	hear	audience

Stems' #6 Test

Name _____ Period _____ Date _____

A. Write the meaning of the following stems.

Stem	Meaning
1. itis	
2. cide	
3. audi	
4. ad	
5. ard	
6. penta	
7. scribe	
8. viv	
9. cred	
10. cede	

B. Write the alphabet of the definition beside the correct word.

Words	Definitions
____ 1. regicide	a. to go back or away from a limit or a point
____ 2. inscribe	b. a star with five points
____ 3. addendum	c. Something added or to be added, especially a supplement to a book
____ 4. recede	d. experiencing something through listening
____ 5. revive	e. one who lingers behind
____ 6. auditory	f. hard to believe
____ 7. laggard	g. the killing of a king
____ 8. pentagram	h. inflammation of a bursa especially on the shoulder or elbow
____ 9. incredulous	i. to be connected to or associated with by a written contract
____ 10. bursitis	j. to return to consciousness or life

19

Stem Bingo (Lessons 4-6)

con	auto	ard
intra	archy	scribe
intro	ician	cede
non	cap	penta
aqua	dict	it is
logy	anthropo	ad
neo	bio	cide
miss	mono	cred
cent	port	viv
cise	bell	audi

Randomly copy one of these stems in each box on your bingo card. Six will not be used.

Copy the Stems Bingo form on the front and back of a piece of paper so the students will have two forms.

Bingo Calling Cards with Definitions
(Lessons 4-6)

together	self	always
= con	= auto	= ard
within	government	write
= intra	= archy	= scribe
into	specialist	go
= intro	= ician	= cede
not	take	five
= non	= cap	= penta
water	say	infection
= aqua	= dict	= itis
science	man	to
= logy	= anthropo	= ad
new	life	kill
= neo	= bio	= cide
send	one	believe
= miss	= mono	= cred
one hundred	carry	life
= cent	= port	= viv
cut	war	hear
= cise	= bell	= audi

Make a copy of this card and cut out the boxes. Shuffle the cards and call out the definitions.

Stems #7

STEM	MEANING	WORD EXAMPLE
hydro	water	hydrant
poly	many	polygamy
hema	blood	hematite
tomy	cut	anatomy
phon	sound	telephone
pseudo	false	pseudonym
omni	all	omnipresent
centri	center	centrist
micro	small	microbiotic
phobia	fear	xenophobia

Stems' #7 Test

A. Write the meaning of the following stems.

Stem	Meaning
1. poly	
2. tomy	
3. pseudo	
4. centri	
5. phobia	
6. micro	
7. omni	
8. phon	
9. hema	
10. hydro	

B. Write the alphabet of the definition beside the correct word.

Words

_____ 1. eccentric

_____ 2. lobotomy

_____ 3. xenophobia

_____ 4. pseudoevent

_____ 5. hematite

_____ 6. omniscient

_____ 7. phonetic

_____ 8. micronize

_____ 9. polychrome

_____ 10. hydroplane

Definitions

a. a mineral constituting an important iron ore that is in a red earthy form

b. not situated at or in the geometric center

c. to pulverize into tiny particles

d. fear of strangers or foreigners

e. decorated with several colors

f. an event that has been faked to engender press coverage and public interest

g. to skim along on the surface of the water

h. having infinite awareness, knowing all

i. of or related to the spoken language

j. the surgical cutting of nerve fibers connecting the frontal lobes of the brain

Stems #8

Stem	Meaning	Word Example
homo	same	homophone
spec	look	spectacles
duct	lead	product
fer	carry	transfer
pend	hang	suspend
photo	light	photograph
vid	look	video
ex	out	exit
re	again	return
hypo	under	hypothesis

Stems' #8 Test

Name _____ Period ____ Date _____

A. Write the meaning of the following stem.

Stem	Meaning
1. vid	
2. hypo	
3. spec	
4. re	
5. homo	
6. photo	
7. pend	
8. fer	
9. duct	
10. ex	

B. Write the alphabet of the definition beside the correct word.

Words

____ 1. spectacles

____ 2. photon

____ 3. homonym

____ 4. pendulum

____ 5. vide

____ 6. ductile

____ 7. exorbitant

____ 8. aquifer

____ 9. hypodermic

____ 10. reiterate

Definitions

a. one of two words spelled and pronounced alike but different in meaning

b. capable of being readily lead or influenced

c. optical instrument consisting of a pair of lenses for correcting defective vision

d. going out of the scope of the law, not in the limits

e. a water carrying stratum of permeable rock, sand, or gravel

f. to state or do over

g. a unit of intensity of light at the retina

h. a body suspended from a fixed point

i. used to direct a reader to look at another item or the next item

j. adapted for use in or administered by injection beneath the skin

Stems #9

STEM	MEANING	WORD EXAMPLE
pan	all	panorama
tele	far	telex
neuro	nerve	neuron
proto	first	protozoa
morph	shape	morphology
vest	clothes	vestibule
bene	good	benefit
pond	weight	ponder
loco	place	locomotive
ortho	straight	orthodontist

Stems' #9 Test

Name _____ Period _____ Date _____

A. Write the meaning of the following stems.

Stem	Meaning
1. loco	
2. pan	
3. vest	
4. tele	
5. bene	
6. pond	
7. ortho	
8. neuro	
9. proto	
10. morph	

B. Write the alphabet of each definition beside the correct word.

Words	Definitions
_____ 1. pantheon	a. unwieldy or clumsy because of weight or size
_____ 2. ponderous	b. one made to resemble a vest and worn under a coat, a dickey
_____ 3. neurology	c. characterized by or suggestive of doing good
_____ 4. mesomorph	d. capable of discerning distant objects
_____ 5. vestee	e. a branch of medicine concerned with the straightening or preventing of skeletal deformities
_____ 6. telescopic	f. a temple dedicated to all gods
_____ 7. benevolent	g. capable of moving independently from place to place
_____ 8. prototype	h. the scientific study of the nervous system
_____ 9. orthopedics	i. an original or first model of something new
_____ 10. locomotory	j. having a husky muscular body shape

Stem Bingo (Lessons 7-9)

hydro	homo	pan
poly	spec	tele
hema	duct	neuro
tomy	fer	proto
phon	pend	morph
pseudo	photo	vest
omni	vid	bene
centri	ex	pond
micro	re	loco
phobia	hypo	ortho

Randomly copy one of these stems in each box on your bingo card. Six will not be used.

Copy the Stems Bingo form on the front and back of a piece of paper so the students will have two forms.

Bingo Calling Cards with Definitions
(Lessons 7-9)

water = hydro	same = homo	all = pan
many = poly	look = spec	far = tele
bolld = hema	lead = duct	nerve = neuro
cut = tomy	carry = fer	first = proto
sound = phon	hang = pend	shape = morph
false = pseudo	light = photo	clothes = vest
all = omni	look = vid	good = bene
center = centri	out = ex	weight = pond
small = micro	again = re	place = loco
fear = phobia	under = hypo	straight = ortho

Make a copy of this card and cut out the boxes. Shuffle the cards and call out the definitions.

Stems #10

Stem	Meaning	Word Example
pop	people	population
nov	new	novel
matri	mother	matron
corp	body	corpse
amphi	both	amphibian
eu	good	eulogy
pater	father	paternity
sangui	blood	sangria
ver	true	verify
dorm	sleep	dormitory

Stems' #10 Test

A. Write the meaning of the following stems.

Stem	Meaning
1. sangui	
2. matri	
3. pop	
4. dorm	
5. ver	
6. nov	
7. pater	
8. eu	
9. corp	
10. amphi	

B. Write the correct letter of each definition beside the word.

Words

_____ 1. verdict

_____ 2. corpuscle

_____ 3. patriarch

_____ 4. populous

_____ 5. matriarch

_____ 6. amphisbaena

_____ 7. novice

_____ 8. euphony

_____ 9. dormant

_____ 10. sanguine

Definitions

a. the oldest male member of a group or family

b. having a large population

c. a serpent in classical mythology having a head at each end and capable of moving in either direction

d. a beginner

e. the finding or decision of a jury based on the facts

f. a pleasing or sweet sound

g. a moderate to strong red

h. inactive

i. a female who rules or dominates a family

j. a living cell of the body

Stems #11

Stem	Meaning	Word Example
tion	act, state	reaction
magn	great	Magna Carta
put	think	impute
mega	large	megaphone
dyna	power	dynamite
octa	eight	octagon
scope	look	telescope
son	sound	sonar
dec	ten	decade
stell	star	stellar

Stems' #11 Test

Name _____ Period ____ Date _____

A. Write the meaning of the following stems.

Stem	Meaning
1. deca	
2. mega	
3. son	
4. tion	
5. magn	
6. scope	
7. dyna	
8. stell	
9. put	
10. octa	

B. Write the alphabet of the definition beside the correct word.

Words	Definitions
_____ 1. magnum opus	a. a tubular optical instrument containing lenses and mirrors in which an observer obtains an obstructed field of view
_____ 2. megalith	b. employed widely or sanctioned by people who think highly of you
_____ 3. dynamometer	c. an apparatus fro measuring mechanical power
_____ 4. octahedron	d. a rough stone used in prehistoric cultures as a monument which was very large
_____ 5. dissonance	e. a contest that has ten different events
_____ 6. interstellar	f. a passage from one stage, subject, state, or place to another
_____ 7. transition	g. the greatest achievement of an artist or writer
_____ 8. periscope	h. located, taking place, or traveling among the stars
_____ 9. decathlon	i. a solid bound by eight plane faces
_____ 10. reputable	j. a mingling of discordant sounds such as clashing or unresolved musical interval or chord

Stems #12

STEM	MEANING	WORD EXAMPLE
demo	people	democracy
stereo	solid	stereotype
cogn	know	recognize
alter	other	alternative
astr	star	astronomy
chron	time	chronic
helio	sun	helios
tetra	four	tetrameter
meter	measure	odometer
amat	love	amity

Stems' #12 Test

Name _____ Period _____ Date _____

A. Write the meaning of the following stems.

Stem	Meaning
1. meter	
2. stereo	
3. cogn	
4. demo	
5. amat	
6. chron	
7. alter	
8. helio	
9. tetra	
10. astr	

B. Write the alphabet beside the correct word.

Words

_____ 1. stereotropism

_____ 2. altruism

_____ 3. synchronize

_____ 4. demography

_____ 5. hydrometer

_____ 6. asterisk

_____ 7. amour

_____ 8. incognito

_____ 9. aphelion

_____ 10. tetrahedron

Definitions

a. an instrument used for measuring the specific gravity of a liquid

b. a polyhedron that has four faces

c. an optical instrument with two eyeglasses for helping the observer to combine the images of two pictures taken from points of view a little way apart and thus to get the effect of solidity or depth

d. a character * used in printing or writing as a reference mark

e. unselfish regard for or devotion to the welfare of others

f. to keep ones identity unknown

g. the statistical study of human populations especially with reference to size and density, distribution, and vital statistics

h. to love

i. to cause to occur or operate with exact coincidence in time or rate

j. the point in the path of a celestial body that is farthest from the sun

Stem Bingo (Lessons 10-12)

pop	tion	demo
nov	magn	stereo
matri	put	cogn
corp	mega	alter
amphi	dyna	astr
eu	octa	chron
pater	scope	helio
sangui	son	tetra
ver	dec	meter
dorm	stell	amat

Randomly copy one of these stems in each box on your bingo card. Six will not be used.

Copy the Stems Bingo form on the front and back of a piece of paper so the students will have two forms.

Bingo Calling Cards with Definitions
(Lessons 10-12)

people = pop	act, same = tion	people = demo
new = nov	great = magn	solid = stereo
mother = matri	think = put	know = cogn
body = corp	large = mega	other = alter
both = amphi	power = dyna	star = astr
good = eu	eight = octa	time = chron
father = pater	look = scope	sun = helio
blood = sangui	sound = son	four = tetra
true =ver	ten = dec	measure = meter
sleep = dorm	star = stell	love = amat

Make a copy of this card and cut out the boxes. Shuffle the cards and call out the definitions.

Stems #13

STEM	MEANING	WORD EXAMPLE
vita	life	vitality
ism	doctrine	capitalism
sur	over	surplus
hyper	over	hyperbole
luna	moon	lunar
gyro	turn	gyrate
contra	against	contradict
geo	earth	geology
thermo	heat	thermostat
prim	first	primary

Stems' #13 Test

A. Write the meaning of the following stems.

Stem	Meaning
1. thermo	
2. sur	
3. prim	
4. vita	
5. luna	
6. hyper	
7. geo	
8. gyro	
9. ism	
10. contra	

B. Write the alphabet of the definition beside the correct word.

Words	Definitions
_____ 1. pluralism	a. the period of time between two successive moons
_____ 2. gyroscope	b. a branch of earth science dealing with physical process and phenomena occurring
_____ 3. thermonuclear	c. the main or first female singer in an opera or concert
_____ 4. viable	d. capable of surviving, growing, or developing life
_____ 5. lunation	e. to become better, greater, or stronger than; to go over what is expected
_____ 6. prima donna	f. a theory or doctrine that there are more than one or more than two kinds of ultimate reality
_____ 7. surpass	g. of or relating to speed five or over five times that of sound in air
_____ 8. contraband	h. a wheel or disk mounted to spin rapidly about an axis
_____ 9. hypersonic	i. illegal or prohibited traffic in goods
_____ 10. geophysics	j. of or relating to the transformation in the nucleus of atoms of low atomic weight that require a very high temperature for their inception

Stems #14

STEM	MEANING	WORD EXAMPLE
tempor	time	temporarily
clam	cry out	exclaim
plu	more	plus
string	bind	stringer
tang	touch	tangent
liber	free	liberty
junct	join	conjunction
soph	wisdom	sophomore
migr	wander	migrate
medi	middle	median

Stems' #14 Test

A. Write the meaning of the following stems.

Stem	Meaning
1. junct	
2. tempor	
3. plu	
4. soph	
5. medi	
6. clam	
7. tang	
8. liber	
9. string	
10. migr	

B. Write the alphabet of the definition beside the correct word.

Words	Definitions
_____ 1. astringent	a. a free thinker especially in religious matters
_____ 2. clamor	b. to add or to join as an accompanying object or circumstance
_____ 3. libertine	c. capable of being precisely identified or realized by the mind
_____ 4. plurality	d. happening, existing, living, or coming into being during the same time period
_____ 5. adjunct	e. able to bind the soft organic tissues as in a lotion
_____ 6. contemporary	f. a search for a general understanding of values and reality or wisdom
_____ 7. migratory	g. roving
_____ 8. tangible	h. being numerous
_____ 9. philosophy	i. of middle or low quality, value, ability, or performance
_____ 10. mediocre	j. noisy shouting

Stems #15

Stem	Meaning	Word Example
clud	close	preclude
se	apart	secret
trib	pay	tribute
dign	worthy	dignify
luc	light	translucent
rupt	break	erupt
grat	pleasing	gratitude
curr	run	current
trans	across	transfer
gamy	marriage	monogamy

Stems' #15 Test

Name _____ Period _____ Date _____

A. Write the meaning of the following stems.

Stems	Meaning
1. grat	
2. luc	
3. gamy	
4. rupt	
5. se	
6. dign	
7. trib	
8. curr	
9. clud	
10. trans	

B. Write the alphabet of the definition beside the correct word.

Words	Definitions
_____ 1. rupture	a. being married to more than one person at a time
_____ 2. gratuity	b. admitting maximum passage of light without diffusion
_____ 3. occlude	c. one who possesses exalted rank or holds a position of honor
_____ 4. pellucid	d. to pay back
_____ 5. incurrent	e. something given for a service well done or to your liking, a tip
_____ 6. polygamy	f. the tearing of a tissue
_____ 7. sequel	g. a part added to a book or play that continues and extends it
_____ 8. dignitary	h. giving passage to a circuit or stream that flows inward
_____ 9. transcend	i. to close or block off
_____ 10. retribution	j. to pass or cross the limits of

Stem Bingo (Lessons 13-15)

vita	tempor	clud
ism	clam	se
sur	plu	trib
hyper	string	dign
luna	tang	luc
gyro	liber	rupt
contra	junct	grat
geo	soph	curr
thermo	migr	trans
prim	medi	gamy

Randomly copy one of these stems in each box on you bingo card. Six will not be used.

Copy the Stems Bingo form on the front and back of a piece of paper so the students will have two forms.

Bingo Calling Cards with Definitions
(Lessons 13-15)

life = vita	time = tempor	close = clud
doctrine = ism	cry out = clam	apart = se
over = sur	more = plu	pay = trib
over = hyper	bind = string	worthy = dign
moon = luna	touch = tang	light = luc
turn = gyro	free = liber	break = rupt
against = contra	join = junct	pleasing = grat
earth = geo	wisdom = soph	run = curr
heat = thermo	wander = migr	across = trans
first = prim	middle = medi	marriage = gamy

Make a copy of this card and cut out the boxes. Shuffle the cards and call out the definitions.

Stems #16

Stem	Meaning	Word Example
numer	number	numeral
fort	strong	fortify
zo	animal	zoology
urb	city	urban
nym	name	acronym
osteo	bone	osteoarthritis
demi	half	demitasse
ego	I	alter ego
voc	voice	vocal
derm	skin	dermatologist

Stems' #16 Test

Name _____ Period _____ Date _____

A. Write the meaning of the following stems.

Stem	Meaning
1. ego	
2. fort	
3. derm	
4. numer	
5. voc	
6. urb	
7. osteo	
8. nym	
9. zo	
10. demi	

B. Write the alphabet of the definition beside the correct word.

Words

____ 1. osteology

____ 2. invoke

____ 3. egocentric

____ 4. epidermis

____ 5. urbanite

____ 6. numerous

____ 7. pseudonym

____ 8. fortitude

____ 9. zombie

____ 10. demigod

Definitions

a. a mythological being who has more power than a mortal but only half of the power as a god

b. strength of mind that enables a person to encounter danger or pain

c. consisting of a great number

d. a branch of anatomy dealing with the bones

e. a pen name or a fake name for someone - usually a writer

f. a person who lives in the city

g. to call forth

h. the outer layer of the skin

i. concerned with only yourself and not others

j. a well-less and speechless figure or animal in the West Indies who is said to have died and came back to life and is capable of only automatic movement

Stems #17

STEM	MEANING	WORD EXAMPLE
leg	read	legendary
tort	twist	tortilla
meta	change	metaphor
hexa	six	hexagon
mir	wonder	miracle
anim	mind	animal
petr	rock	petroleum
volv	roll	involved
sanct	holy	sanctuary
man	hand	manicure

Stems' #17 Test

A. Write the meaning of the following stems.

Stem	Meaning
1. sanct	
2. leg	
3. anim	
4. tort	
5. man	
6. meta	
7. volv	
8. hexa	
9. mir	
10. petr	

B. Write the alphabet of the definition beside the correct word.

Words

_____ 1. mirage

_____ 2. legible

_____ 3. metabolism

_____ 4. animated

_____ 5. petrify

_____ 6. hexapod

_____ 7. manual

_____ 8. contort

_____ 9. revolve

_____ 10. sanctify

Definitions

a. holiness of life or disposition; saintliness

b. to make, design, or produce (a cartoon, for example) so as to create the illusion of motion; giving a mind to something

c. possible to read or decipher

d. having six legs or feet

e. to turn on an axis; rotate

f. an optical phenomenon that creates the illusion of water, often with inverted reflections of distant objects

g. to twist, wrench, or bend severely out of shape

h. done by, used by, or operated with the hands

i. the organic processes or changes that are necessary for life

j. to cause to become stiff or stone-like; deaden.

Stems #18

Stem	Meaning	Word Example
retro	backward	retroactive
sens	feel	sense
ocul	eye	binocular
ultra	beyond	ultraviolet
oid	appearance	asteroid
rid	laugh	ridiculous
lith	rock	lithograph
fract	break	fraction
platy	flat	plateau
fin	end	final

Stems' #18 Test

A. Write the meaning of the following stems.

Stem	Meaning
1. lith	
2. retro	
3. fin	
4. ultra	
5. rid	
6. platy	
7. sens	
8. ocul	
9. fract	
10. oid	

B. Write the alphabet of the definition beside the correct word.

Words

_____ 1. retrogress

_____ 2. ocular

_____ 3. insensate

_____ 4. fracture

_____ 5. finale

_____ 6. derision

_____ 7. platypus

_____ 8. android

_____ 9. ultramarine

_____ 10. megalith

Definitions

a. a semi-aquatic egg-laying mammal of Australia and Tasmania, having a broad flat tail, webbed feet, and a snout resembling a duck's bill

b. from a place beyond the sea

c. relating to the sense of sight

d. a very large stone used in various prehistoric architectures or monumental styles, notably in western Europe during the second millennium B.C.

e. an automaton that is created from biological materials and has the appearance of a human

f. to go or move backward

g. lacking sensibility; unfeeling

h. the act or process of breaking

i. the concluding part, especially of a musical composition

j. contemptuous or jeering laughter

Stem Bingo (Lessons 16-18)

numer	leg	retro
fort	tort	sens
zo	meta	ocul
urb	hexa	ultra
nym	mir	oid
osteo	anim	rid
demi	petr	lith
ego	volv	fract
voc	sanct	platy
derm	man	fin

Randomly copy one of these stems in each box on your bingo card. Six will not be used.

Copy the Stems Bingo form on the front and back of a piece of paper so the students will have two forms.

Bingo Calling Cards with Definitions
(Lessons 16-18)

number = numer	read = leg	backward = retro
strong = fort	twist = tort	feel = sens
animal = zo	change = meta	eye = ocul
city = urb	six = hexa	beyond = ultra
name =nym	wonder = mir	appearance = oid
bone = osteo	mind = anim	laugh = rid
half = demi	rock = petr	rock = lith
I = ego	roll = volv	break = fract
voice = voc	holy = sanct	flat = platy
skin = derm	hand = man	end = fin

Make a copy of this card and cut out the boxes. Shuffle the cards and call out the definitions.

Stems #19

STEM	MEANING	WORD EXAMPLE
ped	foot; child	centipede
carn	flesh	carnivorous
uni	one	unicycle
cor	heart	coronary
jus	law	justice
sol	alone	solo
cant	sing	recant
gyn	woman	gynephobia
nounce	tell	denounce
audro	man	android

Stems' #19 Test

Name _____ Period _____ Date _____

A. Write the meaning of the following stems.

Stem	Meaning
1. gyn	
2. jus	
3. ped	
4. audro	
5. uni	
6. carn	
7. nounce	
8. cor	
9. sol	
10. cant	

B. Write the alphabet of the definition beside the correct word.

Words	Definitions
____ 1. unique	a. a high judicial officer in medieval England
____ 2. pediatrist	b. the condition or practice of having more than one wife at one time
____ 3. carnage	c. a dramatic or literary form of discourse in which a character talks to himself or herself or reveals his or her thoughts without addressing a listener
____ 4. cordial	d. to sing melodiously
____ 5. justiciary	e. to give up (a title, for example) by telling through a formal announcement
____ 6. soliloquy	f. being the only one of its kind
____ 7. renounce	g. corpses, especially of those killed in battle
____ 8. descant	h. a specialist in the care of babies
____ 9. androgens	i. a steroid hormone that controls the development and maintenance of masculine characteristics
____ 10. polygyny	j. warmth and sincerity from the heart; friendly

Stems #20

STEM	MEANING	WORD EXAMPLE
path	feeling	sympathy
nomy	law	astronomy
fid	faith	confidence
co	together	cooperate
hetero	different	heteronym
sci	know	science
graph	write	autograph
lat	side	latitude
tract	pull	tractor
in	in, not	insane

Stems' #20 Test

A. Write the meaning of the following stems.

Stem	Meaning
1. graph	
2. tract	
3. nomy	
4. path	
5. co	
6. in	
7. sci	
8. hetero	
9. fid	
10. lat	

B. Write the alphabet of the definition beside the correct word.

Words	Definitions
____ 1. apathy	a. to draw or pull away; divert
____ 2. taxonomy	b. characterized by being different or departing from accepted beliefs or standards
____ 3. fidelity	c. difficult or not capable to control or manage
____ 4. heterodox	d. the art or process of writing in shorthand
____ 5. omniscience	e. relating to, or situated at or on the side
____ 6. stenography	f. having total knowledge; knowing everything
____ 7. lateral	g. faithfulness to obligations, duties, or observances
____ 8. detract	h. a collaborating or joint author
____ 9. incorrigible	i. lack of emotion or feeling; impassiveness
____ 10. coauthor	j. the science, laws, or principles of classification

Stems #21

Stem	Meaning	Word Example
apt	fit	aptitude
cur	care for	cure
a	not	apathy
phile	love	philosopher
tact	touch	tactful
ambul	walk	ambulance
gest	carry	gesture
fy	make	pacify
theo	God	theology
rect	right	correct

Stems' #21 Test

A. Write the meaning of the following stems.

Stem	Meaning
1. a	
2. ambul	
3. rect	
4. fy	
5. theo	
6. tact	
7. cur	
8. gest	
9. apt	
10. phile	

B. Write the alphabet of the definition beside the correct word.

Words	Definitions

Words

_____ 1. ingest

_____ 2. rector

_____ 3. solidify

_____ 4. curator

_____ 5. maladapted

_____ 6. tactile

_____ 7. amoral

_____ 8. audiophile

_____ 9. atheism

_____ 10. ambulatory

Definitions

a. one who manages or takes care of a museum collection or a library, such as an administrative director

b. perceptible to the sense of touch; tangible

c. to make strong, united, or solid

d. not admitting of moral distinctions or judgments; neither moral nor immoral

e. the doctrine that there is no God or gods

f. a person having a strong interest in stereo, high-fidelity, or audio-sound reproduction

g. to take in and absorb as food so it can be carried through the digestive process

h. capable of walking; not bedridden

i. suited or fit for a particular function or situation

j. to set right; correct

Stem Bingo (Lessons 19-21)

ped	path	apt
carn	nomy	cur
uni	fid	a
cor	co	phile
jus	hetero	tact
sol	sci	ambul
cant	graph	gest
gyn	lat	fy
nounce	tract	theo
audro	in	rect

Randomly copy one of these stems in each box on your bingo card. Six will not be used.

Copy the Stems Bingo form on the front and back of a piece of paper so the students will have two forms.

Bingo Calling Cards with Definitions
(Lessons 19-21)

foot, child = ped	feeling = path	fit = apt
flesh = carn	law = nomy	care for = cur
one = uni	faith = fid	not = a
heart = cor	together = co	love = phile
law = jus	different = hetero	touch = tact
alone = sol	know = sci	walk = ambul
sing = cant	write = graph	carry = gest
woman = gyn	side = lat	make = fy
tell = nounce	pull = tract	God = theo
man = audro	in, not = in	right = rect

Make a copy of this card and cut out the boxes. Shuffle the cards and call out the definitions.

Stems #22

STEM	MEANING	WORD EXAMPLE
lum	light	luminous
ann	year	annual
sess	sit	session
sen	old	senior
bas	low	bass
rogat	ask	interrogation
parl	speak	parlor
potent	power	potential
surg	rise	surge
reg	rule	regiment

Stems' #22 Test

Name _____ Period _____ Date _____

A . Write the meaning of the following stems.

Stem	Meaning
1. potent	
2. reg	
3. lum	
4. sess	
5. surg	
6. sen	
7. bas	
8. parl	
9. rogat	
10. ann	

B. Write the alphabet of the definition beside the correct word.

Words

_____1. insessorial

_____ 2. illuminate

_____ 3. regime

_____ 4. annuity

_____ 5. omnipotent

_____ 6. seniority

_____ 7. parley

_____ 8. basal

_____ 9. derogatory

_____ 10. insurgence

Definitions

a. the action or an instance to rise in the act of rebelling

b. relating to or situated at the lowest level

c. to have a discussion, especially with an enemy.

d. one having unlimited power or authority

e. the state of being older than another or others or higher in rank than another

f. to provide or brighten with light

g. regulated system, as of diet and exercise

h. the yearly payment of an allowance or income

i. disparaging; belittling

j. perching or adapted for perching

Stems #23

Stem	Meaning	Word Example
an	without	anarchy
ab	away	absent
mel	song	melody
bon	good	bonny
struct	build	construct
chlor	green	chlorophyll
mob	move	mobility
gram	writing	telegram
alt	high	altitude
fug	flee	fugitive

Stems' #23 Test

A. Write the meaning of the following stems.

Stem	Meaning
1. fug	
2. an	
3. alt	
4. ab	
5. gram	
6. mel	
7. mob	
8. bon	
9. chlor	
10. struct	

B. Write the alphabet of the definition beside the correct word.

Words	Definitions
_____ 1. refugee	a. any of various unicellular green algae
_____ 2. chlorella	b. not moving; motionless.
_____ 3. bonanza	c. a drama, such as a play, film, or television program, characterized by exaggerated emotions, stereotypical characters, sometimes singing, and interpersonal conflicts
_____ 4. abdicate	d. one who flees in search of a safe place especially in times of war
_____ 5. anemia	e. a condition where the blood is without red blood cells
_____ 6. altimeter	f. to relinquish or give away a high office or responsibility.
_____ 7. monogram	g. an instrument that measures the height above ground
_____ 8. melodrama	h. an underlying base or structure for an organization
_____ 9. immobile	i. a sudden happening that brings good fortune
_____ 10. infrastructure	j. a design composed of one or more letters, typically the initials of a name, used as an identifying mark.

Stems #24

Stem	Meaning	Word Example
gen	origin	gene
nat	born	nation
curs	run	cursive
pre	before	predict
cad	fall	cascade
capit	head	capital
ness	quality	softness
ics	art	graphics
vert	turn	convert
ess	female	lioness

Stems' #24 Test

Name _____ Period _____ Date _____

A. Write the meaning of the following stems.

Stem	Meaning
1. ess	
2. gen	
3. vert	
4. nat	
5. curs	
6. ics	
7. pre	
8. ness	
9. capit	
10. cad	

B. Write the alphabet of the definition beside the correct word.

Words

_____ 1. seamstress

_____ 2. genetics

_____ 3. precursor

_____ 4. inverted

_____ 5. nativity

_____ 6. politeness

_____ 7. prelude

_____ 8. cadence

_____ 9. calisthenics

_____ 10. decapitate

Definitions

a. the event of being born

b. a falling inflection of the voice, as at the end of a sentence

c. to cut off the head of; behead

d. the practice or art of such exercises

e. the genetic makeup or origin of an organism, type, or group

f. the quality of being kind

g. one that runs, precedes, or indicates something to come

h. to turn inside out or upside down

i. a woman who sews, especially one who makes her living by sewing

j. music that comes before the main event of an opera, music that introduces an act in an opera, or part of a book that introduces the book

Stem Bingo (Lessons 22-24)

lum	an	gen
ann	ab	nat
sess	mel	curs
sen	bon	pre
bas	struct	cad
rogat	chlor	capit
parl	mob	ness
potent	gram	ics
surg	alt	vert
reg	fug	ess

Randomly copy one of these stems in each box on your bingo card. Six will not be used.

Copy the Stems Bingo form on the front and back of a piece of paper so the students will have two forms.

Bingo Calling Cards with Definitions
(Lessons 22-24)

light = lum	without = an	origin = gen
year = ann	away = ab	born = nat
sit = sess	song = mel	run = curs
old = sen	good = bon	before = pre
low = bas	build = struct	fall = cad
ask = rogat	green = chlor	head = capit
speak = parl	move = mob	quality = ness
power = potent	writing = gram	art = ics
rise = surg	high = alt	turn = vert
rule = reg	flee = fug	female = ess

Make a copy of this card and cut out the boxes. Shuffle the cards and call out the definitions.

Stems #25

Stem	Meaning	Word Example
aer	air	aerosol
alb	white	album
hum	earth	humble
exo	out	exotic
im	not	impossible
fil	thread	filament
chrom	color	chrome
form	shape	uniform
sequ	follow	sequence
glyc	sweet	glucose

Stems' #25 Test

Name _____Period _____ Date _____

A. Write the meaning of the following stems.

Stems	Meaning
1. glyc	
2. aer	
3. sequ	
4. alb	
5. form	
6. hum	
7. chrom	
8. exo	
9. fil	
10. im	

B. Write the alphabet of the definition beside the correct word.

Words

____ 1. aerobes

____ 2. albino

____ 3. exhume

____ 4. exodus

____ 5. immobile

____ 6. filigree

____ 7. monochrome

____ 8. reform

____ 9. consecutive

____ 10. glycerin

Definitions

a. To remove or take out of the grave; disinter

b. sweet syrupy alcohol obtained by saponification of fats and oils

c. a change for the better; to shape for an improvement

d. a picture, especially a painting, done in different shades of a single color

e. an organism, such as a bacterium, requiring oxygen to live

f. following one after another without interruption; successive

g. delicate and intricate ornamental work made from gold, silver, or other fine twisted wire

h. a departure of a large number of people

i. not moving; motionless

j. a person or animal lacking normal pigmentation, with the result being that the skin and hair are abnormally white or milky and the eyes have a pink or blue iris and a deep-red pupil

Stems #26

STEM	MEANING	WORD EXAMPLE
hemo	blood	hemoglobin
ultima	last	ultimate
milli	thousandth	millimeter
mem	remember	memory
gress	step	progress
labor	work	labored
vac	empty	vacant
ose	sugar	glucose
pod	foot	arthropod
val	worth	valid

Stems' #26 Test

A. Write the meaning of the following stems.

Stem	Meaning
1. ose	
2. val	
3. hemo	
4. milli	
5. gress	
6. vac	
7. pod	
8. mem	
9. ultima	
10. labor	

B. Write the alphabet of the definition beside the correct word.

Word	Definitions

_____ 1. millisecond

a. a final statement of terms made by one party to another

_____ 2. collaborate

b. the qualities of a hero or heroine; exceptional or heroic courage when facing danger

_____ 3. memorandum

c. a very sweet sugar occurring in many fruits and honey

_____ 4. podiatrist

d. to step aside, especially from the main subject in writing or speaking; stray

_____ 5. ultimatum

e. one thousandth (10^{-3}) of a second

_____ 6. valor

f. devoid of expression; vacant or empty

_____ 7. fructose

g. a short note written as a reminder

_____ 8. digress

h. any of several hereditary blood-coagulation disorders in which the blood fails to clot normally

_____ 9. vacuous

i. to work together, especially in a joint intellectual effort

_____ 10. hemophilia

j. the branch of medicine that deals with the diagnosis, treatment, and prevention of diseases of the human foot

Stems #27

STEM	MEANING	WORD EXAMPLE
punct	point	puncture
ject	throw	eject
dox	opinion	doxology
endo	within	endoskeleton
germ	vital, related	germinate
greg	group	segregate
mar	sea	marina
ornith	bird	ornithology
polis	city	metropolis
fus	pour	infuse

Stems' #27 Test

A. Write the meaning of the following stems.

Stems	Meaning
1. endo	
2. ornith	
3. ject	
4. polis	
5. dox	
6. punct	
7. greg	
8. germ	
9. fus	
10. mar	

B. Write the alphabet of the definition beside the correct word.

Words

____ 1. paradox

____ 2. megalopolis

____ 3. endoplasm

____ 4. germicide

____ 5. acupuncture

____ 6. maritime

____ 7. projectile

____ 8. transfusion

____ 9. ornithologist

____ 10. congregate

Definitions

a. an vital agent that kills germs

b. a procedure using fine needles to pierce the body for therapeutic purposes or to relieve pain

c. relating to marine shipping or navigation

d. a fired, thrown, or otherwise propelled object

e. the branch of zoology that deals with the study of birds

f. a statement contrary to received opinion

g. transferring whole blood or blood products from one individual to another

h. to bring or come together in a group, crowd, or assembly

i. the inner portion of the cytoplasm of a cell

j. a region made up of several large cities and their surrounding areas in sufficient proximity to be considered a single urban complex

Stem Bingo (Lessons 25-27)

aer	hemo	punct
alb	ultima	ject
hum	milli	dox
exo	mem	endo
im	gress	germ
fil	labor	greg
chrom	vac	mar
form	ose	ornith
sequ	pod	polis
glyc	val	fus

Randomly copy one of these stems in each box on your bingo card. Six will not be used.

Copy the Stems Bingo form on the front and back of a piece of paper so the students will have two forms.

Bingo Calling Cards with Definitions
(Lessons 25-27)

air = aer	blood = hemo	point = punct
white = alb	last = ultima	throw = ject
earth = hum	thousandth = milli	opinion = dox
out = exo	remember = mem	within = endo
not = im	step = gress	vital, related = germ
thread = fil	work = labor	group = greg
color = chrom	empty = vac	sea = mar
shape = form	sugar = ose	bird = ornith
follow = sequ	foot = pod	city = polis
sweet = glyc	worth = val	pour = fus

Make a copy of this card and cut out the boxes. Shuffle the cards and call out the definitions.

Stems #28

Stem	Meaning	Word Example
spir	breathe	respiration
dia	across	diagonal
acr	sharp	acrid
culp	blame	culprit
per	through	perception
pac	peace	pacify
necro	death	necrotic
brev	short	brief
pugn	fight	impugn
acro	high	acrobat

Stems' #28 Test

Name _____ Period _____ Date _____

A. Write the meaning of the following stems.

Stem	Meaning
1. acr	
2. pugn	
3. brev	
4. necro	
5. spir	
6. pac	
7. culp	
8. acro	
9. per	
10. dia	

B. Write the alphabet of the definition beside the correct word.

Words

_____ 1. expire

_____ 2. pacifism

_____ 3. exculpate

_____ 4. diameter

_____ 5. perforation

_____ 6. necropolis

_____ 7. acerose

_____ 8. oppugn

_____ 9. brevity

_____ 10. acrophobia

Definitions

a. to clear someone of guilt or blame

b. a series of holes punched through paper or some other material so it can be separated easily when tearing it on this line of holes

c. to oppose, to go against as to fight for something

d. a fear of heights

e. when one is against violence and believes in peace

f. it's a straight line drawn across a circle connecting one side to the other side creating a line of symmetry of the circle

g. brief in duration

h. a cemetery that is usually large and elaborate and belongs to an ancient city

i. needlelike, narrow, long and pointed as in pine needles

j. when a person breathes their last breath

Stems #29

STEM	MEANING	WORD EXAMPLE
ecto	outer	ectozoa
plasto	molded	plastic
agog	leader	synagogue
cle	small	molecule
il	not	illegal
ine	nature of	canine
-ar	relating to	solar
hedron	sided object	polyhedron
ous	full of	glorious
topo	place	topic

Stems' #29 Test

Name _____ Period ____ Date _____

A. Write the meaning of the following stems.

Stem	Meaning
1. cle	
2. il	
3. hedron	
4. ecto	
5. -ar	
6. agog	
7. topo	
8. ous	
9. plasto	
10. ine	

B. Write the alphabet of the definition beside the correct word.

Words

____ 1. plaster

____ 2. crystalline

____ 3. particle

____ 4. linear

____ 5. ectoderm

____ 6. vivacious

____ 7. illegible

____ 8. topographical

____ 9. demagogue

____ 10. heptahedron

Definitions

a. relating to a line

b. a leader of the common people in ancient times

c. a paste-like substance used to create a wall, fix holes in a wall, or to create a mold of something

d. a seven faced polyhedron

e. a tiny portion or speck

f. can not be read or figured out

g. having the nature of or composed of a crystal or crystals

h. a map showing the surface features of places or regions

i. the outer layer of a two germ layered animal, such as a jellyfish

j. full of animation and spirit; lively

Stems #30

STEM	MEANING	WORD EXAMPLE
mort	death	mortuary
psych	soul	psychology
ethno	race, culture	ethnic group
paleo	old	Paleolithic
crypt	hidden	cryptic
loqu	talk	dialogue
sacro	holy	sacred
ate	cause	create
muta	change	mutant
apo	away, up	apology

Stems' #30 Test

Name _____ Period ____ Date _____

A. Write the meaning of the following stems.

Stem	Meaning
1. muta	
2. ethno	
3. loqu	
4. ate	
5. mort	
6. apo	
7. paleo	
8. crypt	
9. psych	
10. sacro	

B. Write the alphabet of the definition beside the correct word.

Words

____ 1. crypt

____ 2. soliloquy

____ 3. mortician

____ 4. apogee

____ 5. ethnology

____ 6. sacrament

____ 7. mutation

____ 8. psychic

____ 9. insinuate

____ 10. paleography

Definitions

a. a formal religious act conferring a specific grace on those who receive it

b. the science that analyzes and compares human cultures

c. speaking to yourself

d. the study of ancient forms of writing

e. an alteration or change, as in nature, form, or quality

f. a cellar or burial vault sometimes hidden or beneath a church

g. to cause or introduce a thought in a subtle manner

h. a person whose job is to manage funerals

i. the point farthest away or the highest

j. relating to the mental processes

Stem Bingo (Lessons 28-30)

spir	ecto	mort
dia	plasto	psych
acr	agog	ethno
culp	cle	paleo
per	il	crypt
pac	ine	loqu
necro	-ar	sacro
brev	hedron	ate
pugn	ous	muta
acro	topo	apo

Randomly copy one of these stems in each box on your bingo card. Six will not be used.

Copy the Stems Bingo form on the front and back of a piece of paper so the students will have two forms.

Bingo Calling Cards with Definitions
(Lessons 28-30)

breathe = spir	outer = ecto	death = mort
across = dia	molded = plasto	soul = psych
sharp = acr	leader = agog	race, culture = ethno
blame = culp	small = cle	old = paleo
through = per	not = il	hidden = crypt
peace = pac	nature of = ine	talk = loqu
death = necro	relating to = -ar	holy = sacro
short = brev	sided object = hedron	cause = ate
fight = pugn	full of = ous	change = muta
high = acro	place = topo	away, up = apo

Make a copy of this card and cut out the boxes. Shuffle the cards and call out the definitions.

Stems #31

STEM	MEANING	WORD EXAMPLE
log	word, reason	dialogue
pro	forward	provide
ag	to do	agree
aden	gland	adenoid
fic	make	fiction
ase	enzyme	permease
epi	on	epidermis
-be	life	microbe
cyan	blue	cyanide
diplo	double	diplomacy

Stems' #31 Test

Name _____ Period ____ Date _____

A. Write the meaning of the following stems.

Stems	Meaning
1. pro	
2. aden	
3. fic	
4. epi	
5. cyan	
6. log	
7. ase	
8. -be	
9. ag	
10. diplo	

B. Write the alphabet of the definition beside the correct word.

Words

____ 1. luciferase

____ 2. prognosis

____ 3. adenoma

____ 4. aerobe

____ 5. monologue

____ 6. cyanosis

____ 7. fortification

____ 8. diplopia

____ 9. agitate

____ 10. epigraph

Definitions

a. an organism requiring oxygen to sustain life

b. an inscription, as on a statue or building

c. a medical prediction; forecast

d. an enzyme present in the cells of bioluminescent organisms

e. a long speech made by one person, often monopolizing a conversation

f. the act of making something strong

g. double vision

h. a benign epithelial tumor having a glandular origin and structure

i. to upset; disturb

j. a bluish discoloration of the skin and mucous membranes resulting from inadequate oxygenation of the blood

Stems #32

Stem	Meaning	Word Example
act	to do	action
cyt	cell	cytology
dys	bad	dysfunction
eco	house	economy
emia	blood	anemia
enter	intestine	dysentery
erythro	red	crythrism
idio	peculiar	idiot
infra	beneath	infrared
leuko	white	leukemia

Stems' #32 Test

Name _____ Period ____ Date_____

A. Write the meaning of the following stems.

Stem	Meaning
1. cyt	
2. eco	
3. enter	
4. idio	
5. dys	
6. leuko	
7. erythro	
8. infra	
9. act	
10. emia	

B. Write the alphabet of the definition beside the correct word.

Words

____ 1. cytoplasm

____ 2. enteritis

____ 3. ecosystem

____ 4. crythrocyte

____ 5. activate

____ 6. idiom

____ 7. dysphonia

____ 8. infrasonic

____ 9. toxemia

____ 10. leukemia

Definitions

a. having or relating to a frequency beneath the audibility range of the human ear

b. inflammation of the intestinal tract

c. white blood cells

d. a system formed by the interaction of a community of organisms with their physical environment

e. a condition in which the blood contains toxins produced by body cells at a local source of infection or derived from the growth of microorganisms

f. the protoplasm outside the nucleus of a cell

g. red blood cells

h. to set in motion; make active or more active

i. a style or manner of expression peculiar to a given people

j. difficulty in speaking, usually evidenced by hoarseness

Stems #33

Stem	Meaning	Word Example
phyll	leaf	chlorophyll
pleo	more	pleonasm
soror	sister	sorority
-a	plural	data
para	beside, near	parable
dom	rule	dominate
erg	work	energy
rhiz	root	rhizoid
sapro	rotten	saprolite
schizo	divide	schizm

Stems' #33 Test

Name _____ Period _____ Date _____

A. Write the meaning of the following stems.

Stem	Meaning
1. -a	
2. dom	
3. erg	
4. para	
5. phyll	
6. pleo	
7. rhiz	
8. sapro	
9. schizo	
10. soror	

B. Write the alphabet of the definition beside the correct word.

Words

____ 1. pleomorphic

____ 2. ergonomics

____ 3. rhizome

____ 4. paraphrase

____ 5. phyllopod

____ 6. schizocarp

____ 7. dominion

____ 8. saprophytic

____ 9. sororize

____ 10. trivia

Definitions

a. a horizontal, usually underground stem that often sends out roots and shoots from its nodes

b. an organism, especially a fungus or bacterium, that grows on and derives its nourishment from dead or decaying organic matter

c. any of various branchiopod crustaceans having swimming and respiratory appendages that resemble leaves

d. to associate, or hold fellowship, as sisters; to have sisterly feelings

e. the occurrence of two or more structural forms during a life cycle, especially of certain plants

f. plural of trivium

g. a dry dehiscent fruit that at maturity splits into two or more parts each with a single seed

h. the applied science of equipment design, as for the workplace, intended to maximize productivity by reducing operator fatigue and discomfort

i. a self-governing nation

j. rewording as near to the original for the purpose of clarification

Stem Bingo (Lessons 31-33)

log	act	phyll
pro	cyt	pleo
ag	dys	soror
aden	eco	-a
fic	emia	para
ase	enter	dom
epi	erythro	erg
-be	idio	rhiz
cyan	infra	sapro
diplo	leuko	schizo

Randomly copy one of these stems in each box on your bingo card. Six will not be used.

Copy the Stems Bingo form on the front and back of a piece of paper so the students will have two forms.

Bingo Calling Cards with Definitions
(Lessons 31-33)

word, reason = log	to do = act	leaf = phyll
forward = pro	cell = cyt	more = pleo
to do = ag	bad = dys	sister = soror
gland = aden	house = eco	plural = -a
make = fic	blood = emia	beside, near = para
enzyme = ase	intestine = enter	rule = dom
on = epi	red = erythro	work = erg
life = -be	peculiar = idio	root = rhiz
blue = cyan	beneath = infra	rotten =sapro
double = diplo	white = leuko	divide = schizo

Make a copy of this card and cut out the boxes. Shuffle the cards and call out the definitions.

STEM	MEANING	WORD EXAMPLE
tox	poison	toxin
sect	cut	section
zygo	yoke	zygote
zym	ferment	enzyme
dors	back	dorsal
phos	light	phosphorus
gon	angle	pentagon
vore	eating	carnivore
holo	whole	hologram
opia	sight	biopsy

Stems' #34 Test

A. Write the meaning of the following stems.

Stem	Meaning
1. zygo	
2. tox	
3. zym	
4. vore	
5. holo	
6. dors	
7. gon	
8. sect	
9. opia	
10. phos	

B. Write the alphabet of the definition beside the correct word.

Words

____ 1. dissect

____ 2. zymology

____ 3. holistic

____ 4. tetragon

____ 5. toxic

____ 6. herbivore

____ 7. dorsum

____ 8. zygodactyl

____ 9. myopia

____ 10. phosphoresce

Definitions

a. emphasizing the importance of the whole and the interdependence of its parts

b. to persist in emitting light

c. to cut apart or separate

d. an animal that feeds chiefly on plants

e. the back

f. a four-sided polygon with four angles

g. a science that deals with fermentation

h. having two toes projecting forward and two projecting backward, as certain climbing birds such as a parrot

i. of, relating to, or caused by a toxin or other poison

j. a visual defect in which distant objects appear blurred because their images are focused in front of the retina rather than on it; nearsightedness

Stems #35

Stem	Meaning	Word Example
quin	five	quintuplet
pter	wing	helicopter
spor	seed	spore
sta	stop	station
let	little	booklet
cardio	heart	cardiology
vol	will	volunteer
frat	brother	fraternity
trich	hair	trichina
gno	know	diagnosis

Stems' #35 Test

Name _____ Period ____ Date _____

A. Write the meaning of the following stems.

Stem	Meaning
1. gno	
2. quin	
3. trich	
4. pter	
5. frat	
6. spor	
7. vol	
8. sta	
9. cardio	
10. let	

B. Write the alphabet of the definition beside the correct word.

Words

____ 1. stationary

____ 2. quintet

____ 3. gnostic

____ 4. pterosaur

____ 5. trichosis

____ 6. piglet

____ 7. cardiac

____ 8. volition

____ 9. sporophyte

____ 10. fraternal

Definitions

a. a little pig

b. any disease of or affecting the hair

c. not capable of being moved; fixed

d. the spore-producing or seed producing phase in the life cycle of a plant that exhibits alternation of generations

e. the power or faculty of choosing; the will

f. any of various extinct flying reptiles

g. a composition for five voices or five instruments

h. of or relating to brothers

i. relating to, or possessing intellectual or spiritual knowledge

j. a person with a heart disorder

Stems #36

Stem	Meaning	Word Example
somn	sleep	insomnia
quadr	four	quadrant
cata	down	catacombs
lingu	tongue	bilingual
mot	move	motor
nav	ship	navy
flect	bend	reflect
coron	crown	coroner
aur	gold	aurora
rat	think	rational

Stems' #36 Test

A. Write the meaning of the following stems.

Stems	Meaning
1. cata	
2. mot	
3. quadr	
4. coron	
5. aur	
6. lingu	
7. nav	
8. somn	
9. rat	
10. flect	

B. Write the alphabet of the definition beside the correct word.

Words

____ 1. quadrilateral

____ 2. catapult

____ 3. motile

____ 4. inflection

____ 5. somniloquy

____ 6. navigable

____ 7. coronation

____ 8. linguist

____ 9. auriferous

____ 10. rationalize

Definitions

a. moving or having the power to move spontaneously

b. the act or habit of talking in one's sleep

c. a military machine for hurling missiles, such as large stones or spears, used in ancient and medieval times

d. able to be sailed on or through safely

e. a person who speaks more than one language

f. containing gold

g. a polygon having four sides

h. to think in a rational or rationalistic way

i. a turning or bending away from a course or position of alignment

j. the act or ceremony of crowning a sovereign or the sovereign's consort

Stem Bingo (Lessons 34-36)

tox	quin	somn
sect	pter	quadr
zygo	spor	cata
zym	sta	lingu
dors	let	mot
phos	cardio	nav
gon	vol	flect
vore	frat	coron
holo	trich	aur
opia	gno	rat

Randomly copy one of these stems in each box on your bingo card. Six will not be used.

Copy the Stems Bingo form on the front and back of a piece of paper so the students will have two forms.

Bingo Calling Cards with Definitions
(Lessons 34–36)

poison = tox	five = quin	sleep = somn
cut = sect	wing = pter	four = quadr
yoke = zygo	seed = spor	down = cata
ferment = zym	stop = sta	tongue = lingu
back = dors	little = let	move = mot
light = phos	heart = cardio	ship = nav
angle = gon	will = vol	bend = flect
eating = vore	brother = frat	crown = coron
whole = holo	hair = trich	gold = aur
sight = opia	know = gno	think = rat

Make a copy of this card and cut out the boxes. Shuffle the cards and call out the definitions.

Appendix

Stem Form

Stem Lesson # ____

Stems	Meaning	Word Example

Stem Lesson # ____

Stems	Meaning	Word Example

Stem Lesson # ____

Stems	Meaning	Word Example

Stem Bingo

FREE

Stem Tests' Answers

Stem's #1 Test
A. 1. without
2. seller
3. heavy
4. away
5. book
6. sun
7. wood
8. vapor
9. red
10. like
B. 1. h
2. c
3. j
4. g
5. d
6. a
7. e
8. f
9. i
10. b

Stem's #2 Test
A. 1. after
2. bad
3. before
4. not
5. half
6. three
7. under
8. together
9. over
10. together
B. 1. e
2. h
3. a
4. j
5. d
6. i
7. c
8. f
9. g
10. b

Stem's #3 Test
A. 1. before
2. against
3. two
4. around
5. together
6. down
7. equal
8. beyond
9. between
10. bad
B. 1. d
2. a
3. h
4. e
5. i
6. b
7. g
8. c
9. f
10. j

Stem's #4 Test
A. 1. new
2. within
3. one hundred
4. together
5. cut
6. water
7. send
8. science
9. into
10. not
B. 1. e
2. b
3. j
4. a
5. b
6. i
7. c
8. f
9. d
10. g

Stem's #5 Test
A. 1. one
2. government
3. take
4. specialist
5. self
6. man
7. war
8. say
9. carry
10. life
B. 1. f
2. h
3. a
4. b
5. i
6. j
7. d
8. c
9. e
10. g

Stem's #6 Test
A. 1. infection
2. kill
3. hear
4. to
5. always
6. five
7. write
8. life
9. believe
10. go
B. 1. g
2. i
3. c
4. a
5. j
6. d
7. e
8. b
9. f
10. h

Stem's #7 Test
A. 1. many
2. cut
3. false
4. center
5. fear
6. small
7. all
8. sound
9. blood
10. water
B. 1. b
2. j
3. d
4. f
5. a
6. h
7. i
8. c
9. e
10. g

Stem's #8 Test
A. 1. look
2. under
3. look
4. again
5. same
6. light
7. hang
8. carry
9. lead
10. out
B. 1. c
2. g
3. a
4. h
5. i
6. b
7. d
8. e
9. j
10. f

Stem's #9 Test
A. 1. place
2. all
3. clothes
4. far
5. good
6. weight
7. straight
8. nerve
9. first
10. shape
B. 1. f
2. a
3. h
4. j
5. h
6. d
7. c
8. i
9. e
10. g

Stem's #10 Test
A. 1. blood
2. mother
3. people
4. sleep
5. true
6. new
7. father
8. good
9. body
10. both
B. 1. e
2. j
3. a
4. b
5. i
6. c
7. d
8. f
9. h
10. g

Stem's #11 Test
A. 1. ten
2. large
3. sound
4. act; state
5. great
6. look
7. power
8. star
9. think
10. eight
B. 1. g
2. d
3. c
4. i
5. j
6. h
7. f
8. a
9. e
10. b

Stem's #12 Test
A. 1. measure
2. solid
3. know
4. people
5. love
6. time
7. other
8. sun
9. four
10. star
B. 1. c
2. e
3. i
4. g
5. a
6. d
7. h
8. f
9. j
10. b

Stem's #13 Test
A. 1. heat
2. over
3. first
4. life
5. moon
6. over
7. earth
8. turn
9. doctrine
10. against
B. 1. f
2. h
3. j
4. d
5. a
6. c
7. e
8. i
9. g
10. b

Stem's #14 Test
A. 1. join
2. time
3. more
4. wisdom
5. middle
6. cry out
7. touch
8. free
9. bind
10. wander
B. 1. e
2. j
3. a
4. h
5. b
6. d
7. g
8. c
9. f
10. i

Stem's #15 Test
A. 1. pleasing
2. light
3. marriage
4. break
5. apart
6. worthy
7. pay
8. run
9. close
10. across
B. 1. f
2. e
3. i
4. b
5. h
6. a
7. g
8. c
9. j
10. d

Stem's #16 Test
A. 1. I
2. strong
3. skin
4. number
5. voice
6. city
7. bone
8. name
9. animal
10. half
B. 1. d
2. g
3. i
4. h
5. f
6. c
7. e
8. b
9. j
10. a

Stem's #17 Test
A. 1. holy
2. read
3. mind
4. twist
5. hand
6. change
7. roll
8. six
9. wonder
10. rock
B. 1. f
2. c
3. i
4. b
5. j
6. d
7. h
8. g
9. e
10. a

Stem's #18 Test
A. 1. rock
2. backward
3. end
4. beyond
5. laugh
6. flat
7. feel
8. eye
9. break
10. appearance
B. 1. f
2. c
3. g
4. h
5. i
6. j
7. a
8. e
9. b
10. d

Stem's #19 Test

A.
1. woman
2. law
3. foot, child
4. man
5. one
6. flesh
7. tell
8. heart
9. alone
10. sing

B.
1. f
2. h
3. g
4. j
5. a
6. c
7. e
8. d
9. i
10. b

Stem's #20 Test

A.
1. write
2. pull
3. law
4. feeling
5. together
6. in, not
7. know
8. different
9. faith
10. side

B.
1. i
2. g
3. g
4. b
5. f
6. d
7. e
8. a
9. c
10. h

Stem's #21 Test

A.
1. not
2. walk
3. right
4. make
5. God
6. touch
7. care for
8. carry
9. fit
10. love

B.
1. g
2. j
3. c
4. a
5. i
6. b
7. d
8. f
9. e
10. h

Stem's #22 Test

A.
1. power
2. rule
3. light
4. sit
5. rise
6. old
7. low
8. speak
9. ask
10. year

B.
1. j
2. f
3. g
4. h
5. d
6. e
7. c
8. b
9. i
10. a

Stem's #23 Test

A.
1. flee
2. without
3. high
4. away
5. writing
6. song
7. move
8. good
9. green
10. build

B.
1. d
2. a
3. i
4. f
5. e
6. g
7. j
8. c
9. b
10. h

Stem's #24 Test

A.
1. female
2. origin
3. turn
4. born
5. run
6. art
7. before
8. quality
9. head
10. fall

B.
1. i
2. e
3. g
4. h
5. a
6. f
7. j
8. b
9. d
10. c

Stem's #25 Test

A.
1. sweet
2. air
3. follow
4. white
5. shape
6. earth
7. color
8. out
9. thread
10. not

B.
1. e
2. j
3. a
4. h
5. i
6. g
7. d
8. c
9. f
10. b

Stem's #26 Test

A.
1. sugar
2. worth
3. blood
4. thousandth
5. step
6. empty
7. foot
8. remember
9. last
10. work

B.
1. e
2. i
3. g
4. j
5. a
6. b
7. c
8. d
9. f
10. h

Stem's #27 Test

A.
1. within
2. bird
3. throw
4. city
5. opinion
6. point
7. group
8. vital, related
9. pour
10. sea

B.
1. f
2. j
3. i
4. a
5. b
6. c
7. d
8. g
9. e
10. h

Stem's #28 Test

A.
1. sharp
2. fight
3. short
4. death
5. breathe
6. peace
7. blame
8. high
9. through
10. across

B.
1. f
2. e
3. a
4. f
5. b
6. h
7. d
8. c
9. g
10. i

Stem's #29 Test

A.
1. small
2. not
3. sided object
4. outer
5. relating to
6. leader
7. place
8. full of
9. molded
10. nature of

B.
1. c
2. g
3. e
4. a
5. i
6. j
7. f
8. h
9. b
10. d

Stem's #30 Test

A.
1. change
2. race, culture
3. talk
4. cause
5. death
6. away, up
7. old
8. hidden
9. soul
10. holy

B.
1. f
2. c
3. h
4. i
5. b
6. a
7. e
8. j
9. g
10. d

Stem's #31 Test

A.
1. forward
2. gland
3. make
4. on
5. blue
6. word, reason
7. enzyme
8. life
9. to do
10. double

B.
1. d
2. c
3. h
4. a
5. e
6. j
7. f
8. g
9. i
10. b

Stem's #32 Test

A.
1. cell
2. house
3. intestine
4. peculiar
5. bad
6. white
7. red
8. beneath
9. to do
10. blood

B.
1. f
2. b
3. d
4. g
5. h
6. i
7. j
8. b
9. e
10. c

Stem's #33 Test

A.
1. plural
2. rule
3. work
4. beside, near
5. leaf
6. more
7. root
8. rotten
9. divide
10. sister

B.
1. e
2. h
3. a
4. j
5. c
6. g
7. i
8. b
9. d
10. f

Stem's #34 Test

A.
1. yoke
2. poison
3. ferment
4. eating
5. whole
6. back
7. angle
8. cut
9. sight
10. light

B.
1. c
2. g
3. a
4. f
5. i
6. d
7. e
8. h
9. j
10. b

Stem's #35 Test

A.
1. know
2. five
3. hair
4. wing
5. brother
6. seed
7. will
8. stop
9. heart
10. little

B.
1. c
2. g
3. i
4. f
5. b
6. a
7. j
8. e
9. d
10. h

Stem's #36 Test

a.
1. down
2. move
3. four
4. crown
5. gold
6. tongue
7. ship
8. sleep
9. think
10. bend

B.
1. g
2. c
3. a
4. i
5. b
6. d
7. j
8. e
9. f
10. h

Bibliography

Thompson, Michael Clay. *The Word Within The Word.* Vol. 1. (Royal Fireworks Press, 1998).

Dictionary.com. http://dictionary.reference.com. (Lexico Publishing Group, LLC, 2006.)